# PHANTASY
## AND OTHER POEMS

ETHEL ARCHER (1885-1962), the daughter of a clergyman, was born in Sussex, and expelled from school at the age of fourteen for asking questions in Scripture class. In 1908 she married the aspiring artist Eugene Wieland, and lived with him in West London. The couple made the acquaintance of Aleister Crowley, joined his A∴A∴ magical organization, and set up a publishing company called Wieland and Co., to publish Crowley's periodical *The Equinox*, as well as other texts, including Archer's first poetry collection *The Whirlpool* (1911). She published two other books, *Phantasy and Other Poems* (1930) and the occult novel *The Hieroglyph* (1932).

ETHEL ARCHER

# PHANTASY
## AND OTHER POEMS

THIS IS A SNUGGLY BOOK

This edition Copyright © 2023 by Snuggly Books.

ISBN: 978-1-64525-144-6

This Snuggly Books Edition is an unabridged, slightly amended version of that which was pubished by the Vine Press in 1930.

# CONTENTS

*Preface* / 7

## PHANTASY
Argument / 17
Introduction / 21
Phantasy / 27
To the Moon Spirit / 37
Epilogue / 43

## POEMS
Sleep / 49
Christmas Eve / 53
The Felon Flower / 57
Spring Song / 63
Reverie / 67
Midsummer Morn / 71
Silence / 75
A Song / 79
Suggested by the Music of
   Cyril Rootham's "Brown Earth" / 83
Legend / 87

Vision / 91
In Limine / 95
Hymn to Allah / 99
Victimae Paschali / 105
The Hymn of St. Francis Xavier / 109
Relativity / 113

# INTRODUCTION

IN presenting this Volume to the public some few words of explanation appear to be necessary. This selection covers a wide period of literary activity and is thus indicative of widely varying points of view—from that of *The Felon Flower*, written at the age of sixteen, and some very much earlier poems, to that of the recent translations from the Latin. Similarly, *Phantasy*, which was commenced before the War, and continued after the lapse of several years, indicates a spiritual pilgrimage from Pantheism to Panintheism.

Perhaps in passing I may draw attention to the complex pattern of the rhymes in *Sleep* and *Midsummer Morn*.

Several of the poems have appeared in the *English Review* and other magazines, to whose editors I gladly tender the usual acknowledgements.

*Phantasy* and the *Hymn to Allah* have been set to music by the well-known composer, Miss Dorothy Godwin-Foster, whose address may be obtained from the Vine Press.

It has been suggested that the poems are more likely to be appreciated after a second or even a third reading—if possible aloud—and the reader is asked to suspend his judgment of them until then.

ETHEL ARCHER.

London, S. W.
   March, 1930.

# PHANTASY
AND OTHER POEMS

To
LORD DUNSANY,
to whose Encouragement
this Poem
owes its Completion.

# PHANTASY

A Music Masque and Dream Pageant

# ARGUMENT

THE writer falls asleep in a wood at dusk. During his sleep a thunderstorm comes on, and his dream is peopled with the beings of ancient phantasy.

The really active spirits are Pan and his followers, and these all unconsciously influence the other phantoms of his dream. Thus, when the Pan-pipes are playing merrily, the people of the Court are happy: when the strains are softer and slower, they become sad.

Throughout the dream the fairy music continues, taking him from the Court of Phantasy, where the Knight "Romance" dallies with his faire ladye, back to the woodland, where he sees two lovers who have strayed away from the rest, and is their wanderings have caught Pan sleeping. The god vanishes, but the transitory glimpse has taught them to solve his mystery by solving the mystery of themseives.

This realised, they are returning happily homewards when they come in contact with the other people of the Court.

These, (each separately aware of his own guilt), are talking scandal, to the accompaniment of the envious elves and the swaying hemlock, until the whole wood has become darkened with their malice. Thus, temporarily, the music stops.

But the happy lovers, immortalised through their grand discovery; having disarmed hate and suspicion, a strange and wondrous silence ensues. This is broken by the youngest poet of the Court of Phantasy, "One who from the crowd has wandered, thinking thoughts of Love and Sorrow". In a two-fold Hymn to Luna he voices the thoughts and aspirations of the enlightened crowd. The Hymn dies away in an amplified echo from the distance, this echo enlarging the theme.

The sleeper is awakened at Dawn by the tinkling of a distant sheep-bell.

# INTRODUCTION

I WANDERED out at dew-fall,
And alone
Heard the soft-soughing of the dusk-clad pines
Sink to a shuddering whisper;
Till anon,
The blue-cowled lightning struck the quivering shade,
Waking the thousand images of Eld
That slumbered.
Weirdly-wise
Troop they un-numbered from the listening dells
Of snake-infested silence.
Charmed bells
Tinkle a wondrous music as they go,
Like to the frozen melody that wells
From the thin-reeded river.
Joyous elves
Dance with abandon in the cumbrous shade
Of monstrous gnomes,
(Whose lurching gait they mimic),
Whilst there swells
A changeless, changing rhythm,

Wherein dwells,
Recurring ever, (as the faëry spells
Got of long ages),
One frail glass-like note.

Across the forest carpeted with pine,
Within the shadow of the mighty elms,
The strange sound drew me, till,
Crouched in the hollow of an old, old oak,
Found I an agëd Pan,
Playing upon a pipe of river reeds.
His long beard blew
Over his fingers, as their magic drew
The old enchantment; till the dryads ran,
Laughing, to meet him; and the elfin crew,
Hid i' the branches, mischief great did plan.

The lucid mantle of the large-eyed moon
Lay in its golden glamour over all;
How daintily they let the fir-cones fall!
Laughing to see them roll, as children do;
And all the while the magic murmur grew,
For Pan was merry on this night of June!

Into the forest stepping silently
Came haughty ladies from a
Court long dead,
Talking in dulcet tones to lords who bled
Years since in battle, duel, or some fray
Wrought by the amorous god.

How blithely gay
Seems now their converse, tripping jauntily,
Now falling sadly, as the music strays
In softer mood, even as the player plays.

For Pan they see not, though the fairy glade
Throng with his followers. Their stiff brocade
Rustles no louder though some winsome sprite
Lurk in the folds, who laughing tries to bite
The coral ear wherefrom some jewel weighs,
Stirring to envy all his heart's delight.

They know not whence that sylvan music springs,
Touching the triple chord of ecstasy;
Nor yet the passing memory it brings,
Fraught with the soul of all the woodland things
Born in the night.

They only feel the subtle sorcery
Of summer madness, when the tangled hair
Of some bright nymph has caught them unaware,
Adding her kisses to the dimpled breeze,
Laughing to Pan deep hid within the trees,
Still playing, playing, to the summer air.

O magic night of Love and Secrecy!
Soft stars are trailing through the amber dusk,
A nameless mystery surrounds the husk
Of life new-breaking. O the sapphire sea
Pearled with its foam of stars!

The crystal key
Whereof who holds, knows not
Life's anarchy.

I watched from out the shadows warily,
And marked the passing pageant as it flowed
In rhythmic wonder down the winding road:
The darkened forest—monstrous effigy
Of Simian dwarfs with twisted limbs, that flee
The moving shadows till the darkness grows
One phosphor flame, more frail than elfin snows
Wherein I founder. Swiftly, silently,
The dream clouds o'er me, as a limpid sea
Of gloom-voiced laughter, echoing eerily,
Fades in the distance.
Endlessly it flows,
This strange procession, as some spiral goes,
And I must follow, whither no man knows.

# PHANTASY

So, to that ancient Court, where Phantasy,
Sleeps in the moonlight, and the knight Romance,
Visored and plumed, and armed for errantry,
Haunts yet the dewy sward. His charger, gay
With silken trappings, champs impatiently,
Pawing the lawn, the while for one last glance
His master lingers. Can his lady say
When next their meeting? Whether far away
In some fell foreign land, or where the may
Powders the hedge rows? But the silence knows;
And, gravely gay, she kisses tenderly
The wild wet rose; then throws it to him. They,
The Sisters Three, shall surely guard him! Nay,
*Must* guard him. So, they part. And still the strain
Of fairy music echoes. As a flute
Silverly-sweet, the fountain tumbles. Mute,
The shadows hasten to the marble brim,
Melting in mist, and merge themselves; or float
Like argent lilies on a mystic moat
Guarded by moon-beams. For the fairies' whim
Is ever to seem beautiful, and feign

Beauties they know not of, so they may chain
All beauty to them. So I dreamed.
                              Again,
Lost in the aureole of the moon's bright hair,
I saw two Lovers turning. Deathly fair
Were their pale features, for a glad despair
Born of too strange a knowledge kept them there,
Lured by the forest, that for days had known
Their sweet communion. Silently, alone,
Through the vast wood they wandered, and at morn
Had found the Wood-God sleeping. Round him, torn,
Lay scattered leaves and flower garlands. Torn
Was his goatish beard, and likewise torn
The floating garment of some wood-nymph—(born
Say of what midnight struggle!)—for her hair,
Fragrant as dawn and light as gossamer,
Lay yet within his grasp. The astonished pair
Scarce caught the vision ere the monster woke,
Saw them, and vanished. And before them, there,
Grey in the sunshine, was an aged oak,
Crabbed, gnarled, and rotten,—the decaying stem
Covered with mossy growths; and binding them,
Just where one limb protruded, hung a haze,
Silv'ry and fine—a silken spider's maze.
So still they wander seeking him: and Night
Follows the Day, and from her azure steep
The Moon looks down and loves them; and soft Sleep
Weaves them her poppied mantle, and they creep
Deep down within the folds, and oft-times weep
For very happiness of dear delight.

Once more a vision; and the fountain-court
Is filled with lords and ladies, and the sport
Of whispering elves and mannikins is fraught
With dire intention. Sinister with Thought
The pine trees shiver. In the listening gloom
Pale ghostly moths flit phantom-wise, and loom

Silent as ashen Fate, whose eyes' still doom
Sees in the mouldering Past the Future's tomb,
Nor waits for any man. The gold-orbed Moon,
(A luminous void within the indigo),
Droops down behind the trees, whose gaunt arms trace
Sad violet sigils that the winds embrace,
Scattering the fallen leaves. About the place
Like vast dim echoes of the worlds' great race,
Rung from the chains of inter-stellar space
Circling immensity. Then silence, so
My heart may hear its beating, and I know
Not what of fell interpretation lends
Itself to my soul's secrecy, and blends
All loftier magic with that still small rune.
But I am silent, and I mark the tune
Of the silver showers of the fountain, and the swoon
Of the great silver stars, as each one bends
In lofty adoration, and descends
To bathe in her own beauty; and the tears
Of all the fettered phantasms of years
Seem subtly intermingling in the whirl
Of this strange Universe, whose voices curl

In blind "fantastic nautch'; till Darkness furl
The flags of the wind, and down the ravine hurl
The tattered hosts. So, to oblivion.
Then, 'mid the shadow of the dreaming yews,
Strange Night-Shapes gather; and pale ghastly dews
Drip from their ice-cold fingers, to infuse
With deadly malison the woodland round.
The deadly night-shade steals from out the ground,
And the lank hemlock casts its fatal flower
About the ivied slopes, where seems to cower
The ancient memory of evil things,
The Formless and the Misbegotten. Wings,
Bat-like and envious, beat the lowering air
In ever lessening circles, (as Despair,
That shapes but its own orbit, yet must dare
Endlessly to escape, the while aware
Of its own impotence.) An awful glare
Lights up the woodland, as each guilty pair
Halts in mid-darkness, seeming to declare
The other's thought: then, feigning ignorance,
Each keeps the narrow circle, moving on
At the same pace: the one ignoble fear
Goading all minds in secret, that they share
Their neighbour's haunt. O hateful variance
Of Truth with Custom, Reason with Romance!
Courage, as virtue, reaps her fair reward;
Virtue, as cowardice, is rightly scored:
And ye are cowards all, yet each must taunt
With trivial spite the other, so to vaunt

---

\* This phrase is borrowed from V.B.N.

Better his perfect self. And so they walk,
Whispering scandal, to the poisoned talk
Of envious elves, whose council is to balk
All human happiness. And yet more near
The tall shapes gather, and a new-born fear,
Creeping by stealth amid the listening trees,
Stirs in their topmost branches. Ill at ease
The faint leaves rustle, as they strive to share
The winds' low secret.

        As a bird of sable plumage
        Rising from a stormy ocean,
        Sweeps the Night across the hill-tops;
        Ruffled are his shining feathers,
        All his wings are dashed with water,
        Drops which falling dull earth's torches,
        Drown the stars in all their glory:
        Then the pale-faced moon in terror
        Draws a veil across her features,
        Bows her weeping head in silence,
        Praying for the stars, her children.
        But the Night recks naught of sorrow,
        Scornfully he rushes onward,
        Shakes anew his gloomy pinions,
        While his yellow eyes dart lightning.
        From his cave beneath the mountains
        Warily the Sun-God watches,
        Shakes his crested head in anger,
        Fixes flaming eyes upon him;
        Yet the Night draws on undaunted.

In the distance, through the darkness,
From without the whirling tempest,
Comes the sound of happy voices,
Sweetest sounds of sweeter converse,
Love confessed to Love's Confessor:
And the steadfast pair returning,
Touched not by the storm around them,
Tell a tale of wondrous beauty,
Tell a tale whereon they marvel,
While the light of a great gladness
Rests upon their happy faces:
Thus they sing, the youthful Lovers,
Love brought safely through the Darkness.

"Far within the distant woodland
We have found the great Pan sleeping,
And in vanishing he left us
For the greater God Who made him;
And a knowledge all transcendent
Lighteth up the world around us:
We have found the inmost meaning
Of the sun-beam and the dew-drop,
Of the hush of winds at evening,
And the pleasant summer pastures;
Love alone is of God's nature,
Wherefore true love must be God-like,
And the love of meanest creature
Adds but to His praise and glory;
Each within the other, finding
Image of himself transcended,
Knows at last the greater union

Wherein all things must be blended;
Finds his God, and God instructs him:
Love alone is key to all things,
Earthly love, the pale reflection
Of that greater Love whose glory
Fills the earth and floods the Heaven;
Of that greater Love whose glory
Seen alone on earth would blind us;
Yet we seek it; ever turning
Strife to Life, and darkness spurning."

Then upon that sombre woodland,
Full of sounds of whispered malice,
Falls a strange and wondrous silence,
Sweeter than the sound of harp-strings,
Than the distant sound of harp-strings,
Than the memory of music
When the heart for love is silent.
And one, youngest of the poets,
Foundling of the Court of Fancy,
One who from the crowd has wandered,
Thinking thoughts of love and sorrow,
Lifts his child-clear voice to Heaven,
With his child-pure brow adoring,
Making songs of fair entreaty
To the white-veiled Queen of Heaven,
And the whole wide wood is silent.

# TO THE MOON SPIRIT

"OH bright and glorious Spirit, born of the air,
Thou angel-guardian of the silver moon,
That read'st with solemn awe her mysteries,
And, like the Jewish patriarch of old
Stand'st on the Threshold dread with veilëd face,
Fearful to show mankind its auguries:
Remove the cloud that hides thee from my gaze!
Reveal thyself in beauty, heavenly rare,
And give me insight to the mystery
Surrounds thy radiant being, and the key
That access gives to that bright spirit world
Whose god-like speech strikes not dull mortal ears.
Say what thy mind doth pass, as, through the night,
The windswept clouds are tossed about thy brow,
The pale gold orb o'er Earth and Heaven doth shine,
And all around is peace most loneliest?
What fearful secret lock'st thou in thy breast?
What vague unholy terrors dost thou see,
Whilst looking down with calm benignant eye
Upon the still and sleeping earth beneath?
Say, ever does mankind in wildest thought

Think thou art witnessed of all their deeds,
Or that thy bright and dazzling face is dulled
By looking on their crime and misery?
To man thou speak'st not, but perchance to God
Thou tell'st a mingled tale of joy and woe,
Reflected in thine own all-glorious face
To mortal eyes which seems so passionless.
If this be so, thou need'st must know the fate
Impending on our one and every deed;
And, as thou roamest through the worlds of space,
With prophet eye foresee our destiny.
But only, glorious Spirit, give to me
The power to sing thy praises far and wide,
And I renounce all vain ambition else,
And, as thy chaunter, I am satisfied.

"O Luna, who, when Night's black shadow, creeping
Like some dark vision, doth the world enfold,
Dost shed thy silver light whilst stars are peeping,
And earth's round orb onward in space hath roll'd;
O Luna, beautiful, pure, fair, and stately,
What poet hath not of thy praises sung?
What wanderer lone hath not been gladdened greatly
When thou in Heaven hast like a lantern hung,
And pointed out to him his homeward way,
And where-through all the shades of Night it lay?

"O Luna fair, what hast thou not beholden
From thy high throne in Heaven's cloudless space,
When thou hast watched until the sunlight golden
Hath filled each babbling brook and shady place?

What bloody battlefields hast thou looked down on?
What paramours have met beneath thy light?
What naiads of the wood with myrtle crown on
Have danced and sported all the livelong Night?
Till Dawn hath come, and they have fled way,
For nymph and naiad ne'er are seen by day.

"O Queen of Heaven! Look down on every nation,
And let thy gentle peace steal in our heart;
Teach the whole world with all the blest creation
To know, and each to do, his destined part.
Set us thy pure example, that, thee seeing,
Upward to higher regions may we soar,
Beyond the thought and sight of mortal being,
Where mortal man hath never trod before;
Teach us to gladly know the one true Will,
And whilst on earth we live, pursue it still."

   *(Distant echo.)*
"The one true Will, to which all wills be turn
The Vision of the Universe, set free
From Adam's curse. Pan and his nymphs returning
Back to the woods; and fairest minstrelsy
Limning the earth."

   *(Fainter still,*
   *but very clear.)*
"All things a manner of our mode of seeing, And
Love the quest and answer to our Being."

# EPILOGUE

SOFT is the brooding Doves whose love-swift wings
From the high heaven sped downward, when of old
She saw, and seeing, loved the King of Kings,
Shadowing His sacred head from the fierce heat;
So dies the song. And swift the morning's gold
Spreads slowly.
On the hills the dew is sweet.

The silent voices of the Dawn
Are waking round me, Life is still;
And Death in transport seems as Life,
The Higher Servant of the Will:
I know not if I die or live,
Or if I move or cease to be,
Save only that within my heart
Lies Love's untrammelled ecstasy.

## POEMS

# SLEEP

ALONG the siver pathways of the moon,
(With lilies strewn to mark her passing hours),
A mighty goddess strays.
Her rapt eyes gaze in calm undying swoon,
Like stars in June that guard Barth's sleeping flowers,
The guests of summer days.
Moving, she plays some sweetly-slumbrous tune
As mothers croon; through faint Acollan showers
Her mist-hung garment sways.

And in her shadow, 'chaste as starlit snows',
A vestal goes, scattering sweet roses,
Roses deep-thorned and red,
Whose leaves are shed in perfumed dreams, where glows
A world that blows, and fairy-like discloses
The fields that Flora fled.
And some are sped where dream brings that repose
The thorn bestows—(where nought that is, reposes)—
Goring the sleeper's head.

# CHRISTMAS EVE

PEACEFUL calm upon the waters,
  Gentle stillness o'er the wave,
Orient stars like Beauty's daughters
All the world with splendour lave.
And the moon in stately glory
Drives her silver car along,
Till the earth, with frost still hoary,
Bursts at daybreak into song.

# THE FELLON-FLOWER
## (A RHAPSODY)

As the sighing of souls that are waiting the close of the light,
As the passionate kissings of Love in the Forest of Night,
As the swish of the wavelets that beat on a cavernless shore,
Or the cry of the sea-mew that echoes a moment or more,
So the voice of thy spirit soft-calling my soul in its flight.

As the breath of the wind that is borne from the island of Love,
As the swift-moving cloudlets that sail in the heaven above,
As the warmth of the sunlight that breaks on the shimmering sea,
And the sweetness that lurks in the sting of the honey-fed bee,
So the joy of thy kiss, the dread offspring of serpent and dove.

As the trail of the fiery lightnings which gleam in the
    dark,
As the light from the measureless Bow of the
    seven-fold Arc,
As the fires which glance o'er the face of the
    treacherous deep,
When none but the furies may rest, and the nereids
    weep,—
So thy meteor eyes, brightest sirens alluring Love's
    barque.

When hid in the wonderful maze of thy whispering
    hair,
Alone with the shadows and thee, and away from the
    glare
Of the burning and pitiless day, and the pitiless light,—
Thee only beside me, above me the mystical night,
No dream so created in darkness was ever more fair.

For then was thy touch as the light of a life-giving fire,
Which kindles, and scorches, and burns, with
    unsated desire,
Thy breath the warm essence of myrtle, the fragrance
    of pine,
The languorous smoke of a temple *obscene yet divine,
Which gladdens the soul of a god in his passionate ire.

So silent those nights, I could fancy the uttermost deep
Engulfed us for ever,—for ever in silence to keep

---

\* 'Obscene' in the sense of pagan.

The tale of our wooing: till sweetly the murderous hours
Had lulled us to rest; and the magical poison of flowers
Had stolen our brains, and our eyelids were heavy
    with sleep.

Ah love! They are banished, yet not so the strength
    of the spell
Which holds both our beings in bondage, a bondage
    so fell
That even the angels above cannot alter its power;
It lives in the memory yet of one passionate hour,
When from the dark bosom of Hell sprang a fair
    felon flower.

# SPRING SONG

KISS me pretty maiden.
With the loose brown hair,
That, with sorrow laden,
I thy joy may share.

Draw with fond caresses
Me from self apart.
Through thy waving tresses
Smile with guileless art.

When my wayward glances
Ardently do burn,
As the blush enhances
Shyly from me turn.

On the downy pillow
Of thy yielding breast,
From Life's surging billow
Let me be at rest.

All thy youthful brightness
Let not sorrow mar,
With a laugh of lightness
Chase my gloom afar.

Through thy veiling lashes
(Like the forest deer)
When my dark eye flashes
Glance with sweetest fear.

As the crimson flowers
Of thy lips I press,
Ere thy soft glance lowers
With an answer bless.

Then with hearts enlightened,
Hand in hand we'll roam,
Each with soul love-brightened
Through the woodlands, home.

# REVERIE

WHEN NIGHT unbinds her shadowy hair
And starlight glimmers o'er the wave,
And grey old Neptune seeks his lair
Within some wan and lonely cave,
While dreaded Darkness silent stalks
Where'er the storm-fiends maddest rage,
Unfettered, the dim spectre walks,
The memory of a vanished age!

When sweet-browed Solitude reveals
The April-radiance of her face,
And o'er the west the crimson steals
In many a varied form of grace,
Upon the whispering wind is borne
Soft music from a world at rest,
And rustling garments sweep the corn,
Or stir the foaming billow's crest.

But when Aurora softly shakes
Her golden tresses bathed in dew,
And o'er the East the sunlight breaks

In spear-like rays of sparkling hue,
Upon the mirrored waves is cast
An Image, that to Death is wed,
Then fades; a shadowy form has passed
The harrowing dream of hopes long dead.

# MIDSUMMER MORN

WARILY the watchful shadows guard alone the
    ambush'd green;
Till a whisper faintly dawning, fills the fragrant air of
    morning,
Like a vague unuttered warning to a host of
    Things Unseen.
Then the dewdrops glance and glisten on the leaves
    the fairies christen,
Whilst the still air strives to listen to their laughter
    sweet and keen.

From the silent shores of Midnight hath the dancing
    Day withdrawn;
And I long to tread the measure of her never-tiring
    pleasure,
Such as men and maids did treasure ere the troubled
    Fates were born;
And with soul but newly saddened, I would seek the
    joys that gladden'd,
And the many songs that madden'd all the minstrels
    of the morn.

But in vain from dusk to dawning, once the wondrous quest begun,
Do I plead with love unspoken for the fragile fairy token
That shall bear my spirit broken to the Lands beyond the Sun;
Yet when Hope herself seems lying, I may find it still undying,
In some Land, with sleep slow-sighing, where our deeds and dreams are one.

# SILENCE

AMID the thunder of the rolling spheres,
Herself unchanged despite the changing years,
    She stands supreme, alone.
With trembling hands tight pressed to rigid ears,
Deaf to all prayers, and hopes, and human tears,
One voiceless Horror-louder than all fears,
    Filling the great Unknown.

# A SONG

THE light mind dallies within the deep,
　The wanton waves are far from home,
And like a poppy-petal, sleep
Lies on the silken-bearded foam.
And near at hand the sea-maids comb
Their amber tresses; and I creep
Within the golden net, and weep
For all the lesser loves that roam.

**SUGGESTED BY THE MUSIC
OF CYRIL ROOTHAM'S
"BROWN EARTH"**

MYSTERY,
The mystery of eternal birth,—
And the brown Earth,
Slowly shaping, breathing, called into being.
. . . . . . . . . . . . . .
Immensity of silence,
Cold stars, blackness,
And the brown Earth growing.

The brooding calm of the Vast Countenance filling
    the heavens,
Vast forms upon the horizon, majestic, god-like . . . .
A choir of the immortals,
And the brown Earth resting, sleeping.

Spring,
Soft winds, sunshine, the laughter of little children,
And the brown Earth dreaming her dream of summer.

Harmony, beauty, rhythm.
The interplay of cosmic forces,

The magic and the mystery of Life,
Great sweeping curves, of colour, light and sound,
And (as in a dream),
The far-off choir of the immortals,
Growing, nearing, fading away over the horizon,
Into the distance.

# LEGEND

THE castle stands upon a lonely rock,
   Far to the west, where a tempestuous sea
Beats ever to the shoreward, and the wind
Wails in the shroud of many a ghostly ship
Lured to its doom by a strange minstrelsy.
A magic music floating from the tower
When nights are blackest, and the mighty deep
Holds strange enchantment: so the moon doth cower
Behind a cloud, the sun and stars do sleep,
The daylight dies—yet nothing doth expire,
For Nothing wholly is—(Nothing we know—
We know not what that Nothing is we know)—
So dream the mariners drifting, till a shock
Shatters the fragile timbers, as the spray
Scatters the nameless dream. Yet, it may be,
That one strong swimmer, lustier than the rest,
May hear, above the raging hurricane,
The great and awful fury of the gale,
That wondrous melody. The silver sound,
Steals from a flute, within the topmost tower
Of that black fortress, whose unbending brow

Stares frowning o'er the deep.
The iron casement, triple-barred and bound,
Shews no fair prisoner, and the sweet sounds cease
When falls the swimmer. Yea! The sweet sounds cease,
Yet rising once again they lure him on.
He falls and falls again; they lure him still—
He falls for the last time: the music dies—
So none may know its meaning. I have heard,
None but the dead may know it, or a bird
Dying far off from home.
They say, It is the Love-Lament of Death.
Beauteous it is.

# VISION

A SOUND of soft caressing, and the plash
Of little lapping waves about the prow,
Woke him from slumber. In the farthest East
The sun had risen, and the new-born Day,
Resplendent from her couch of gold and pearl,
Bent smiling o'er him. In her azure eyes
Were dreams of heaven, and all things wonderful
Were mirrored in her gaze; and, as she looked,
A Royal city rose from out the sea,
Gleaming like crystal, and the golden light
Spread over all, a wondrous peace and warmth,
And yet no sound,—
But silence as of music manifold.
She led him to the footsteps of the Throne,
All lesser things were banished from his sight,—
The Light that never was on land or sea
Enveloped them.

# IN LIMINE
(Ignotum per Ignotius)

O ROSE of Death, open thy petals wide!
　Aching with infinite sweetnesses within
To crush the wavering insect, and to win
From the deep crimson heart of thee a tide
Of wondrous Life; as when the Crucified,
Hanging in shame to expiate all sin,
Found in the dying thief a soul akin
To His own soul. Is not all Truth allied?
O miracle of miracles sublime,
That all created things should sink to climb!
O mystery incarnate of the soul,
That dies but to be born anew! The whole,
One monstrous effigy of Life, that
Time Scrawls with fantastic hands from pole to pole.

# HYMN TO ALLAH

*Being a free translation of a Hymn by Mirza Guhlam Ahmad of Qadian (1839-1908), founder of the Ahmadyia Muslims whose English headquarters are at Woking in Surrey.*

A LLAH! First Source of Light! How manifest that
Light
      and how perfected.
The mighty Cosmic Plan is but a glass where man,
      sees Thee reflected!
But yesternight the moon drew me into a swoon,
      Thy beauty slew me.
Brightly emblazoned there in Heaven, the soul of her
      who erstwhile knew me.

Yea! For on all sides round proof of Thy Power is found,
      Thy wondrous Power.
The Sunlight waves we see discernible in Thee,
      O mighty Dower.
And each fond earnest star peeping from out the bar
      of Beauty's lashes
Is but a facet dim of that bright Diadem
      Whose light she flashes.

All beauties of the Earth draw and sustain their birth
      from Thy pure passion.

And every garden close bears in its heart the rose
>	Thy love doth fashion.
Each sleepy-eyed gazelle shews where some flow'ret fell
>	when Thou wast dreaming,
And every curl of her curls upward nor shall stir
>	the Light broad-streaming.

Like to a keen-edged sword Thy glance is, O my Lord,
>	all things it severs.
Nor can I live without the sight of Thee, a drought
>	my senses shivers.
And like a sick man yearns the soul of me, and burns
>	my sight to gladden
With the sweet sight of Thee, O wondrous ecstasy
>	the heart to madden.

A thousand veils there be surely to curtain Thee
>	from men of blindness,
Else would Thy face be seen Qibla of all I ween
>	who praise Thy kindness.
Moslem with him who knew not the great Prophet, true
>	yet to His teaching,
Strove upwards to the Light, slaying the hosts of Night
>	with Love far-reaching!

Say! What is this that stirs Earth to her confines, blurs
>	sense in one rapture?
Hasten to comfort me, lest Death, in ecstasy,
>	my Love should capture.

Eyes of my heart have seen, ears heard, (the sense
 between),
  things beyond naming.
Beauty. the whole of her, proves God the soul of her,
  God, the Light flaming.

# VICTIMAE PASCHALI

*Written by the monk Wipo of St. Gall in the 11th century, it is the oldest of the many* liturgical mysteries *which were acted in Church by the clergy as part of the service. The first two parts were sung by the Choir, the third by the Apostles Peter and John, the fourth by the Holy Women, and the fifth by the full Choir again. In this translation the third and fourth parts have been somewhat amplified.*

TO the Paschal Offering
Christians offer praise, and sing:

Christ the Lamb, for sinners slain,
Doth the sheep a ransom gain.
He the Holy, Undefiled,
Man to God hath reconciled.
Death and Life in wondrous wise
Struggle for the Sacrifice.
Christ, the Victim of the strife,
Dying, reigns, the Lord of Life.

"Tell us, Mary, what the sight
Thou sawest ere the morning's light,
As thou wentest to the tomb,
Willed with heavy grief and gloom?"

"I saw the stone, now rolled away,
Two angels bright as burning day;
Their shining robes, than sun more white,
Did turn to day my darkest night;

I saw the place where He had lain,
But not the body of the Slain.
The grave clothes, and the kerchief there—
The angels testimony bare:
'He is not here, your Lord', they said,
'Why seek the Living 'mongst the dead?
Bethink ye, the third day hath come,
And he is risen from the tomb!'—
The Lord our hope is risen, and
He Doth go before to Galilee!"

We would believe the tale of Mary true,
Rather than tales of any false-tongued Jew.
We know, O Victor-King, Thou art risen indeed:
Look down in pity on Thy suppliants' need.

# THE HYMN OF ST. FRANCIS XAVIER

*Being a free translation from the Latin of J. W. Nakatenus (1669). The original, now unhappily lost, was a Portuguese Sonnet written by St. Francis in 1546.*

NOT for reward, and not for punishment,
Not for the fear of death and banishment,
Not for the hope of that high Heaven to be;
The Heaven of Hope, where Love eternally
May feast on Love—nay, Lord, but Thee, but Thee,
Thee I love only, as Thou lovest me,
And I will love Thee ever.

Thou art my King, and for me Thou hast spent
Hard years of toil, grief, and discouragement,
For me hast felt the cross, the cruel load
Of falsehood, ignominy, and the flood
Of bitter sorrows, all because of me,
And all for me, a sinner.

Thou art my God, and for me Thou wast slain,
For me, a sinner, Thou didst bear the pain,
For me did'st die, for me did'st rise again,
For me hast conquered Hell and Death and Sin,
For me hast opened Heaven—Thyself to win,
So, Lord, I love Thee as Thou lovedst me.

Can I do aught but love Thee, Lord, most dear,
Thou who from Heaven could'st stoop to light and
The souls of sinful men? Nay, Lord, but hear I
Not for reward, and not for fear of pain
I love Thee, Lord, but for Thyself's sweet gain,
THEE I love only as Thou lovest me.

# RELATIVITY

LEAVE all the Future of your hopes
And wend along the Past with me.
The future vista never opes,
And yet, the best is yet to be.
"To be" and "was" and "is" are—NOW:
Reflect, and thou wilt never stay
To cull the blossoms out of sight,
Or pluck the blooms of yesterday.

# A PARTIAL LIST OF SNUGGLY BOOKS

**ETHEL ARCHER** *The Hieroglyph*
**ETHEL ARCHER** *The Whirlpool*
**G. ALBERT AURIER** *Elsewhere and Other Stories*
**CHARLES BARBARA** *My Lunatic Asylum*
**S. HEZOLNRY BERTHOUD** *Misanthropic Tales*
**LÉON BLOY** *The Tarantulas' Parlor and Other Unkind Tales*
**ÉLÉMIR BOURGES** *The Twilight of the Gods*
**CYRIEL BUYSSE** *The Aunts*
**JAMES CHAMPAGNE** *Harlem Smoke*
**FÉLICIEN CHAMPSAUR** *The Latin Orgy*
**BRENDAN CONNELL** *Metrophilias*
**BRENDAN CONNELL** *Unofficial History of Pi Wei*
**BRENDAN CONNELL (editor)**
  *The Zinzolin Book of Occult fiction*
**RAFAELA CONTRERAS** *The Turquoise Ring and Other Stories*
**DANIEL CORRICK (editor)**
  *Ghosts and Robbers: An Anthology of German Gothic Fiction*
**ADOLFO COUVE** *When I Think of My Missing Head*
**QUENTIN S. CRISP** *Aiaigasa*
**LUCIE DELARUE-MARDRUS** *The Last Siren and Other Stories*
**LADY DILKE** *The Outcast Spirit and Other Stories*
**CATHERINE DOUSTEYSSIER-KHOZE**
  *The Beauty of the Death Cap*
**ÉDOUARD DUJARDIN** *Hauntings*
**BERIT ELLINGSEN** *Now We Can See the Moon*
**ERCKMANN-CHATRIAN** *A Malediction*
**ALPHONSE ESQUIROS** *The Enchanted Castle*
**ENRIQUE GÓMEZ CARRILLO** *Sentimental Stories*
**DELPHI FABRICE** *Flowers of Ether*
**DELPHI FABRICE** *The Red Sorcerer*
**DELPHI FABRICE** *The Red Spider*
**BENJAMIN GASTINEAU** *The Reign of Satan*
**EDMOND AND JULES DE GONCOURT** *Manette Salomon*
**REMY DE GOURMONT** *From a Faraway Land*
**REMY DE GOURMONT** *Morose Vignettes*
**GUIDO GOZZANO** *Alcina and Other Stories*
**GUSTAVE GUICHES** *The Modesty of Sodom*
**EDWARD HERON-ALLEN** *The Complete Shorter Fiction*
**EDWARD HERON-ALLEN** *Three Ghost-Written Novels*

**J.-K. HUYSMANS** *The Crowds of Lourdes*
**J.-K. HUYSMANS** *Knapsacks*
**COLIN INSOLE** *Valerie and Other Stories*
**JUSTIN ISIS** *Pleasant Tales II*
**JULES JANIN** *The Dead Donkey and the Guillotined Woman*
**GUSTAVE KAHN** *The Mad King*
**MARIE KRYSINSKA** *The Path of Amour*
**BERNARD LAZARE** *The Mirror of Legends*
**BERNARD LAZARE** *The Torch-Bearers*
**MAURICE LEVEL** *The Shadow*
**JEAN LORRAIN** *Errant Vice*
**JEAN LORRAIN** *Fards and Poisons*
**JEAN LORRAIN** *Masks in the Tapestry*
**JEAN LORRAIN** *Monsieur de Bougrelon and Other Stories*
**GEORGES DE LYS** *An Idyll in Sodom*
**GEORGES DE LYS** *Penthesilea*
**ARTHUR MACHEN** *N*
**ARTHUR MACHEN** *Ornaments in Jade*
**CAMILLE MAUCLAIR** *The Frail Soul and Other Stories*
**CATULLE MENDÈS** *Bluebirds*
**CATULLE MENDÈS** *Mephistophela*
**ÉPHRAÏM MIKHAËL** *Halyartes and Other Poems in Prose*
**LUIS DE MIRANDA** *Who Killed the Poet?*
**OCTAVE MIRBEAU** *The 628-E8*
**CHARLES MORICE** *Babels, Balloons and Innocent Eyes*
**GABRIEL MOUREY** *Monada*
**DAMIAN MURPHY** *Daughters of Apostasy*
**KRISTINE ONG MUSLIM** *Butterfly Dream*
**OSSIT** *Ilse*
**CHARLES NODIER** *The King of Bohemia and His Seven Castles*
**CHARLES NODIER** *Outlaws and Sorrows*
**HERSH DOVID NOMBERG** *A Cheerful Soul and Other Stories*
**PHILOTHÉE O'NEDDY** *The Enchanted Ring*
**GEORGES DE PEYREBRUNE** *A Decadent Woman*
**HÉLÈNE PICARD** *Sabbat*
**JEAN PRINTEMPS** *Whimsical Tales*
**JEREMY REED** *When a Girl Loves a Girl*
**ADOLPHE RETTÉ** *Misty Thule*
**JEAN RICHEPIN** *The Bull-Man and the Grasshopper*
**FREDERICK ROLFE (Baron Corvo)** *Amico di Sandro*

**JASON ROLFE** *An Archive of Human Nonsense*
**ARNAUD RYKNER** *The Last Train*
**LEOPOLD VON SACHER-MASOCH**
   *The Black Gondola and Other Stories*
**MARCEL SCHWOB** *The Assassins and Other Stories*
**MARCEL SCHWOB** *Double Heart*
**CHRISTIAN HEINRICH SPIESS** *The Dwarf of Westerbourg*
**BRIAN STABLEFORD (editor)**
   *Decadence and Symbolism: A Showcase Anthology*
**BRIAN STABLEFORD (editor)** *The Snuggly Satyricon*
**BRIAN STABLEFORD (editor)** *The Snuggly Satanicon*
**BRIAN STABLEFORD** *Spirits of the Vasty Deep*
**COUNT ERIC STENBOCK** *The Shadow of Death*
**COUNT ERIC STENBOCK** *Studies of Death*
**MONTAGUE SUMMERS** *The Bride of Christ and Other Fictions*
**MONTAGUE SUMMERS** *Six Ghost Stories*
**ALICE TÉLOT** *The Inn of Tears*
**GILBERT-AUGUSTIN THIERRY**
   *The Blonde Tress and The Mask*
**DOUGLAS THOMPSON** *The Fallen West*
**TOADHOUSE** *Gone Fishing with Samy Rosenstock*
**TOADHOUSE** *Living and Dying in a Mind Field*
**TOADHOUSE** *What Makes the Wave Break?*
**LÉO TRÉZENIK** *The Confession of a Madman*
**LÉO TRÉZENIK** *Decadent Prose Pieces*
**RUGGERO VASARI** *Raun*
**ILARIE VORONCA** *The Confession of a False Soul*
**ILARIE VORONCA** *The Key to Reality*
**JANE DE LA VAUDÈRE** *The Demi-Sexes and The Androgynes*
**JANE DE LA VAUDÈRE** *The Double Star and Othe Occult Fantasies*
**AUGUSTE VILLIERS DE L'ISLE-ADAM** *Isis*
**RENÉE VIVIEN AND HÉLÈNE DE ZUYLEN DE NYEVELT**
   *Faustina and Other Stories*
**RENÉE VIVIEN** *Lilith's Legacy*
**RENÉE VIVIEN** *A Woman Appeared to Me*
**ILARIE VORONCA** *The Confession of a False Soul*
**ILARIE VORONCA** *The Key to Reality*
**TERESA WILMS MONTT** *In the Stillness of Marble*
**TERESA WILMS MONTT** *Sentimental Doubts*
**KAREL VAN DE WOESTIJNE** *The Dying Peasant*

www.ingramcontent.com/pod-product-compliance
Lightning Source LLC
Chambersburg PA
CBHW020541080526
44583CB00013B/943